The Eternal Value System
Part 2

By Bob Mumford

P.O. Box 3709 ❖ Cookeville, TN 38502
931.520.3730 ❖ lc@lifechangers.org

For more than 50 years Judith and I have
been family friends with Bob and Jan Sutton.
Bob nurtures the body of Christ as a pastor and
educator. He served many years as an editor of
New Wine Magazine. I would like to express
my gratitude for Bob's assistance in helping me
communicate the Kingdom as it is now emerging.
Thank you, Bob, for your editorial skill, wisdom,
and friendship.

Unless otherwise noted, all Scripture quotations are taken from
The New American Standard Bible, The Lockman Foundation,
1960, 1962, 1963, 1968, 1972, 1973, 1975, 1977. All rights
reserved.

PLUMBLINE

Published by:

P.O. Box 3709 | Cookeville, TN 38502
(800) 521-5676 | www.lifechangers.org

Follow Me:
The Eternal Value System
Part 2

By Bob Mumford

When Jesus asks the Father "not to take us out of the world,"[1] it carries implications that are quite far-reaching. It is exceedingly necessary that we examine and explain Christ and His Kingdom from this presupposition: the world in which we live must be understood and engaged. As we posited in the first *Plumbline* in this three-part series, *Engaging the World*, it became increasingly apparent that we are unable to govern ourselves. Whether it is our own appetites, economies, nations, environment, or the entire international community, our systems of governments have proved ultimately ineffective in producing harmony and justice within the increasingly unstable climate of the global culture. Governance, from the perspective of our Lord Jesus, is not in the form of government but in the value system underlying the government. External systems are limited in their effectiveness. They are essentially unable to transform an increasingly corrupt culture governed by values of a fallen mindset.

Through the *Basilea* [Kingdom] of God's eternal spiritual government we find a light at the end

1   John 17:15

of the tunnel. God's *Basilea* is expressed in God's eternal value system, which is not merely a standard of ethical behavior but rather the very governmental expression of His Agape nature—God IS Agape. It may increase the emphasis on "not being taken out of the world" when we recognize that Matthew alone uses the concept of the Kingdom 54 times in the very first book of the New Testament.

Our value systems govern our judgments, our choices, and our priorities—no exceptions! On a basic level everything and everyone is governed by one of two internal, spiritual value systems. These value systems are not merely codes of behavior; they are spiritual forces that permeate everything they touch. The most pervasive value system in modern culture is the eros value system. There are seven foundational motivations of the fallen mind-set that are rooted in eros, the Seven Giants:

1. Look good
2. Feel good
3. Be right
4. Stay in control
5. Hidden agenda
6. Personal advantage
7. Remain undisturbed

The bottom line of the eros value system is to please myself at any time and for any reason.

The primary value system is rooted in Agape. It is the expression of God's very nature—the MO by which He relates to and governs the entire cosmos and all of human kind. There are four expressions of God's Agape:

1. I will keep my word.

2. I will not encroach on that which is another's.

3. I will look for an opportunity to do you good.

4. If I cannot do you good, I want you to know My intent is not to do you harm.

First, God's faithfulness to His word[2] is the absolute foundation of our faith. Without this assurance all else in meaningless. We may rest on the faithfulness of His character: He is the same yesterday, today, and forever. With Him there is no variation or shifting shadow.

The consummation of His sovereign purpose in the redemption and reconciliation is utterly dependent on a single promise made to Abraham, "In your

2   Please note that I am using "word" rather than "promises" as I did in the first *Plumbline, Engaging the World.* His word includes His promises but is more explicit of God's whole nature and character. Word (especially *logos* in the New Testament) denotes the expression of thought that embodies a concept or idea. As I use it in relation to the eternal value system, it is the expression of who God declares Himself to be and in keeping His word about Himself there is no changing, uncertainty, or ambiguity. Because of His character His promises are certain. "I AM that I am."

seed will all the families of the earth be blessed."[3]

Second, even though Creator God has the right as the absolute Sovereign by right of creation, He will not usually encroach on human sovereignty. He holds us humanly responsible to choose how our lives are to be governed. As much as we might desire Him to ride in on His white horse and clean up our mess, He has left the ball in our court. He extends the offer of His Kingdom, but He does not mandate that we accept it. His desire is for mature sons and daughters who respond from love, not prisoners or robots.

Third, He is looking for opportunities to do us good. Because God *is* good, He can only *do* good. However, beyond that, God is not capriciously good—He is aggressively good. How often have we been overjoyed by the comfort of His presence, an unexpected financial blessing, an answer to a long-forgotten prayer, or the favorable resolution of a seemingly disastrous situation. God's desire to do us good is not because of any obligation on His part; rather, out of joy He is looking for opportunities to express His Agape. It is critical that we remember that Father's good for us may not fit the definition of good as we would like to imagine it. This we will unpack more fully as we proceed.

Fourth, God wants us to understand that it is never His intent to harm us. How contrary this is to the picture painted by religion showing God as

---

3   Genesis 22:18

angry and waiting, fire and lightening kindled and ready to meet out vengeance on the world for offending Him. Jesus seeks to correct this perverted understanding.

Governing ourselves by the eros value system has proven through millennia of human history to be futility. We have believed the gospel carries in it the message of hope to a hurting world. However, the "gospel" we have too often presented is a marketing scheme which says, "Accept Jesus, your sins will be forgiven, He'll make everything right, and you get to go to heaven when you die." The gospel I believe Jesus presented is: *"God has a government, why don't you try it*!" It is a government expressed in His eternal value system.

If we consider the eternal value system as the only value system sufficient to undergird the government of our inhabited world, how do we get there? We cannot and will not make a new set of "Kingdom rules," which we won't ultimately accept or keep because of the influence of our fallen mindset. We quickly realize we *cannot DO* the eternal value system, but *we must BECOME* the eternal value system. Jesus did not just teach the eternal value system, He was the incarnational demonstration of it. We are not capable of making this incarnational transformation in and of ourselves. The Father has prepared a custom made pathway for our transformation that we must seek to embrace with singularity of purpose. To this end Jesus makes the Kingdom offer: *Follow Me!*

Introduction

Mincaye was an Auca Indian of the Huaorani tribe in the jungles of eastern Ecuador. In 1956, he along with several of his fellow tribesmen brutally murdered five Christian missionaries who were seeking to bring the gospel to them. Almost 50 years later, in 1997, he came to the United States as a Christian pastor to share how the gospel had changed the lives of this tribe.

Naturally, the modern, technical world was an amazement to him. Airplanes he could understand because they had wings like the birds. Other things he accepted with wonder. However, as he was led to immigration and customs control, he had to step onto a moving walkway. Here he hesitated. How could a pathway move of its own accord? This was just not possible!

Weeks later he returned to his tribe and was relating all he had seen. They awed and laughed as he shared his experience with airplanes, automobiles, and all the strange things he had seen—until he got to the moving walkway.

"No," they said, "a pathway cannot move by itself!"

"Yes," he insisted, "I'm telling you, the path itself was moving!"

As a people who lived and moved on jungle pathways, this just was not possible.

The Moving pathway

When Judith and I were first married we trained to be medical missionaries among the Auca Indians in eastern Peru. The plans never came to fruition; however, our interest in the Auca people remained, and we took interest in this story. As I related the story to Judith over our kitchen table, her eyes lit up and she remarked, "A moving pathway—that sounds like the Christian life!"

Instantly fireworks went off in my spirit! Is the Christian life actually a moving pathway carrying us along a determined course toward a destiny of the Father's intention? Is He using, and sometimes designing, the flow of events and circumstances in our lives to carry us to a providentially predetermined destination He envisioned for us before the foundation of the world? If a moving pathway is an accurate metaphor for our Christian experience, then we must ask: What is its end? How would that operate? Judith's insight brought new clarity and insight to the reality of our Father's ways.

When Jesus invited the disciples to follow Him, He was issuing a call to something deep within each of them. It was not a call to a new religious discipline, surely they had plenty of that close at hand. It was deep calling to deep, appealing to a subtle, God-given longing for something greater and more transcendent than the mundane routines of fishing and tax collecting. It was a call to a grand adventure and romance that only God can offer. It was a call that ignited a burning in their hearts to leave everything to pursue something they had always longed for but had never known until they encountered Jesus. This is expressed by John Eldredge and Brent Curtis in their wonderful book, *The Sacred Romance:*

> This Sacred Romance is set within all our hearts and will not go away. It is the core of our spiritual journey. Any religion that ignores it survives on as guilt-induced legalism, a set of propositions to be memorized and rules to be obeyed.[4]

If you have heard God's call and responded to Jesus' invitation, "Come, Follow Me", then please consider carefully with me this ever familiar passage:

> And we know that God *causes all things* to work together for good to *those who love* God, to those who are called *according to His purpose*. For those whom He foreknew, He also *predestined to become conformed to the image of His Son*, so that He would be the firstborn among many brethren [Italics mine].[5]

How often I have heard people lightly quote Ro-

---

4   *The Sacred Romance; P. 18.* © 1997 by Brent Curtis and John Eldredge. Thomas Nelson Publishers.

5   Romans 8:28-29

mans 8:28 saying, "God makes everything work out for your best." Carefully reading the entire passage, we must note that "my good" is inexorably tied to the Father's sovereign calling and purpose that is clearly expressed as "becoming conformed to the image of His Son." Father did not send His Son to take on the sin of the world in order that I might live free of pressure and difficulty: to be healthy, wealthy and wise! The destiny of the pathway is each of us becoming mature sons and daughters, living in the eternal value system in the same manner which Jesus did as the firstborn of many sons and daughters.

Let me restate this most succinctly:

> The moving pathway is Father working through "all things," both providential and permitted, conforming us to the image of His Son and thereby reconciling us to Himself.

It is important to note that Paul does not say, "God causes all things [period]. " Rather, He causes "all things to work together." In some mysterious manner God makes room for the operation of darkness; the failure of others; conflicts; and our own failures, stubbornness, and poor choices. In His sovereign transcendence He then causes them to become co-laborers with Him for our growth and progress. We cannot charge the Father with being the source of our conflicts, but we can trust Him to bring resurrection out of death because the Eternal I AM lives by His own eternal value system.

When I accepted the Lord's call to follow Him I was convinced He had given me two goals: win the world for Jesus and convert the entire Church to my Pentecostal doctrines. Through over sixty years of following Jesus it has slowly dawned on me that He has been much more intent on my *becoming* than on my *doing*. He designed a pathway that would work toward His purpose for me rather that my own. This has at times caused exceeding dissonance in my soul when He failed to follow my path and insisted on leading me down His. This cartoon was providentially given to me by my wife, Judith, during the writing of this *Plumbline*. It ever so graphically illustrates my point!

Metaphorically, I think the bicycle on which our little friend is riding could be representative of all cultures and religions. It represents the best of

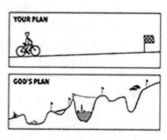

human effort. It is wonderful for making "my plan" work out but totally inadequate for following God's plan! As a matter of fact, my plan will need to be totally abandoned to get where the Father is taking us!

We need the assistance of the One who has successfully navigated this Pathway before us. What is the "Son" image the Father is seeking to form in me? I would like to suggest four characteristics that I believe capture the essence of the Father's desire and purpose.

Firstly, "Son" is a relationship. It is self-evident that a son cannot have being apart from a father. When God spoke to us in (not "through") a Son,[6] He was setting forth the relationship that He seeks with us. It is more important than we imagine—the basis of God's very being and doing is relational.

Everything about Jesus was defined by His relationship with His Father, it was the foremost priority in His earthly life. He was continually poised toward His Father: relying only on what the Father gave; teaching only what He heard from the Father; and doing only what He saw the Father doing—ultimately living only to please His Father. His ministry, both what He taught and what He did, was to present a true image of His Father, which was distorted and perverted by the fallen mindset working through religion. He was the *exact* representation of the Father's being and nature.

Secondly, He was the incarnation of the eternal value system. Jesus lived in and by the eternal value system in His relationship to all He touched. He taught it as the heart of His Father and set it forth as the standard for all who would seek to live within the governmental sphere of Agape.

Thirdly, as the last Adam, Jesus lived as the Son of Man, a genuine human as God intended from the

6   See Hebrews 1:2

beginning. Consider carefully the expression of Romans 8:29 from The Message:

> God knew what He was doing from the very beginning. He decided from the outset to shape the lives of those who love Him along the same lines as the life of his Son. *The Son stands first in the line of humanity He restored. We see the original and intended shape of our lives there in him*[7] [Emphasis mine].

In Jesus, as the Pattern Son, we see the pattern human as God intended from the beginning.

Fourthly, Jesus was the fulfillment of the promise made to Abraham that in his seed (descendants) all the nations of the earth would be blessed[8]. The ultimate redemption and reconciliation of all humanity and all creation are contained in this single promise. A critical part of God's eternal value system is "I will keep My word." His sovereign purpose for all human history has been the realization of this promise to Abraham; Jesus Himself being both the beginning and consummation of its fulfillment.

It is important that we understand being conformed to the image of the Pattern Son engages <u>Father's intention</u> for us to become, like Jesus,

7   THE MESSAGE: The Bible in Contemporary Language © 2002 by Eugene H. Peterson. All rights reserved.

8   Genesis 12:3; 18:18; 22:18. See also Galatians 3:16-19.

an incarnation of the eternal value system. Listen carefully to Jesus as He explains the practical manifestation of the eternal value system to His disciples:

> But I say to you who hear, love your enemies, do good to those who hate you, bless those who curse you, pray for those who mistreat you. Whoever hits you on the cheek, offer him the other also; and whoever takes away your coat, do not withhold your shirt from him either. Give to everyone who asks of you, and whoever takes away what is yours, do not demand it back. Treat others the same way you want them to treat you. If you love those who love you, what credit is that to you? For even sinners love those who love them. If you do good to those who do good to you, what credit is that to you? For even sinners do the same. If you lend to those from whom you expect to receive, what credit is that to you? Even sinners lend to sinners in order to receive back the same amount. But love your enemies, and do good, and lend, expecting nothing in return; and your reward will be great, *and you will be sons of the Most High*; for He Himself is kind to ungrateful and evil men. *Be merciful, just as your Father is merciful*[9] [Emphasis mine].

---

9   Luke 6:27-36.

Jesus told His disciples that as citizens of the Kingdom they were to be, as He was Himself, embodiments of the eternal value system. As such they would be present in the world as light and salt affecting, changing, influencing, and giving life to those they encountered in the world as Jesus did.

In the parallel passage in Matthew, Jesus concludes this very similar discourse by telling His disciples, "Therefore you are to be perfect, as your heavenly Father is perfect."[10] If we are honest in our application of Jesus' command, we are forced to admit the mark is far higher than any of us can hope to reach operating out of a mindset that is primarily self-referential and eros driven. To live authentically in the eternal value system requires *transformation of my very person.* As a life-long Bible teacher and "how to" person, my first inclination would have been to develop a study on seven steps to living the eternal value system. To be perfectly honest, I was thinking that direction as I started to write this until I was brought up short realizing the only pathway to authentic transformation is through a living, dynamic relationship. Following Jesus on the moving pathway recognizes that Jesus does not desire or intend to take us out of the real world.

Many years ago the Lord said to me, "Bob Mumford, you and I are incompatible—*and I don't change!*" This simple phrase allows me to interpret and embrace many of the ways of God in my own

10   Matthew 5:48

life, often enabling me to understand why my best efforts to get God to do it my way usually end in abject frustration. I have increasingly come to understand the purpose of His government working in Bob Mumford is that I might become a living incarnation of His eternal value system expressing His Agape in the same manner Jesus did.

This is expressed quite succinctly by C. S. Lewis, a "long distance" mentor who has fed, nurtured, and guided me for many years:

> To ask that God's love should be content with us as we are is to ask that God should cease to be God: because He is what He is, His love must, in the nature of things, be impeded and repelled by certain stains in our present character, and *because He already loves us He must labour to make us lovable*. We cannot even wish, in our better moments, that He could reconcile Himself to our present impurities [Italics mine]. [11]

Father's "labor to make us lovable" is our custom designed moving pathway. The Father has designed personal pathways to move us towards goals we could never arrive at on our own. As we

---

11   C. S. Lewis; *The Business of Heaven* (p. 12). Harper One. Kindle Edition.

investigate the nature of the moving pathway please engage and rest in the foundation of God's intense Agape for us as individuals. Each member of the Trinity—Father, Christ Jesus, and the Holy Spirit— is committed in Agape to transform us into the image of the Pattern Son and give us full inheritance in the Kingdom of God.

Nature of the Pathway

First, the goal of your own pathway has been predetermined by the Father. When arriving at an airport, if you step on a moving walkway pointing toward the rental car center, don't expect to end up at the baggage claim! Once you are on the moving walkway the rental car center is your predetermined goal no matter how badly you may want to get to the baggage claim. Most of us have been given, or created our own, visions of what our journeys would be like if we gave our lives to Jesus and played by the rules. How shocked we become as we begin to discover God isn't playing by our rules—look again at the little cartoon I shared earlier! We have committed to Jesus as "the Way" and that determines the end result.

No two pathways are the same. Father's design for each of us is uniquely tailored to our own needs and personal calling. It is tempting to compare, contrast, judge, or try to emulate the path others are called to walk. Even though we can learn from the experience of others, we must accept our own pathway as coming from a Father who knows us better than we know ourselves.

Second, the pathway moves at its own pace and events are unpredictable. We cannot accelerate our pathway or stop it. Sometimes it moves at a dizzy speed; other times it seems to jerk to a dead stop. Often it does not seem to move when we most want it to. It can take unpredictable turns or even seem to be going in the wrong direction. Parts of the pathway are sunny, smooth, and the blessings seem to rain out of heaven. Other times the lights go out leaving us feeling fearful, alone, and asking questions. However, do not worry, all things are in His hands.

Third, the illusion that we are in control is a personal delusion. This is not to imply that we are not free to make choices and pursue our own devices. It simply means that events, circumstances, and persons over which and whom we have no control can radically alter or even totally derail our best intentions and direction. Please note the "all things" in Romans 8:28. There is only one way to interpret "all things"—it means *ALL THINGS!*

Within this magnificent repertoire we discover His grace. If we are to progress on the moving pathway, we must embrace God's Agape as so providential that He will bring us to His purpose by employing our own decisions, weaknesses, and failures; and (SHOCK!) we will eventually come to understand that short comings and failures are a necessary part of the process of maturing!

Fourth, the moving pathway is a source of reality, designed to reveal me to me. In revealing me to me He is endeavoring to save me from ME! He confronts my personal sovereignty, which seeks self-preservation expressing itself through the Seven Giants.[12] The pathway functions as the reality in which Christ can reveal to me the hidden things that hinder or injure His image forming within me. Jesus had a habit of leading His disciples into reality checks: "You give them something to eat . . .. Why were you so fearful? . . . Before the cock crows. . .. "

One day I was merrily cruising along the Interstate at 79 (actually 80) MPH. So was everyone else, I was just keeping with the traffic flow. Quietly the Spirit spoke to me, "You are not capable of keeping the speed limit."

I thought briefly about that and said to myself, "Of course I am!" I eased off the accelerator and slowly my speedometer wound down to 70 MPH. Quite contented with myself, I watched other motorists fly by at 80+ MPH. Slowly my impatience began to stir. As the pressure of my frustration grew I gradually transferred that pressure to my right foot on the accelerator. There was a sense of relief when I rejoined the traffic flow as my speedometer progressively crept back to the 80 MPH mark.

12   The Seven Giants: *Look good; feel good; be right; stay in control; hidden agenda; personal advantage, and, remain undisturbed.*

After a few moments the Lord whispered, "See what I mean?"

REALITY CHECK!

The moving pathway confronts my personal sovereignty and reveals with ruthless efficiency the ungoverned desires that keep me from obeying.

Fifth, the moving pathway is transformational. The moving pathway is designed to produce in us a transformation, more accurately a metamorphosis of our value system and person. Metamorphosis is written into the fabric of creation as part of the universal law of death and resurrection. It is breathtaking to watch a humble caterpillar change into a chrysalis and then emerge as a free and magnificent butterfly. The transformation that is predestined for us is just as mysterious and magnificent. Metamorphosis operates as we engage and embrace His purpose in contrast to our own.

Sixth, the moving pathway is a mystery. The complete knowledge of some things, the Father retains for Himself. Mystery is the nature of the Kingdom by God's own choice. It is more a theme of the New Testament than we have dared to realize; "mystery" is mentioned 27 times in the New American Standard translation! Everything will always be a mystery to some extent, and if we are to flow in the realm of the meta-cognitive[13] we must become increasingly comfortable with mystery and learn to

---

13   Defined, *meta-cognitive* sounds like this: "A kind of thinking that is *beyond* or *different* than my own."

live within that context. Mystery is designed to frustrate the legalist and encourage those of us who are seeking to follow Him.

The workings of the Spirit in the "chrysalis of death" between the caterpillar and the butterfly are often veiled from our understanding. Many things that come our way on the moving pathway will not seem to make the least sense in our understanding of how things should be. Sometimes there seems to be no visible connection between an event on the pathway and any beneficial outcome. If we do come to understand, it is most often in retrospect rather than in immediacy. Some things we do not need to know, and if we did know we would not understand. We walk by faith, not by sight.

Seventh, we are not taking this journey alone. I cannot count the number of times I have ministered to someone who confessed to me, "I feel like I'm the only one who . . .." The sense of isolation can sometimes flood our persons when we least expect it. It is in these times that our faith must dig into the bed rock of reality that we are never alone on the journey. Jesus successfully walked the moving pathway and "since He Himself was [tested] in that which He has suffered, He is able to come to the aid of those who are [tested]."[14]

Allow me to be repetitive: the moving pathway is a *relationship* not a rulebook. I cannot emphasize this too urgently. The people of God are over-

---

14   Hebrews 2:18

run with bible texts, to-do lists, principles, steps, and strategies on how to live victoriously. None of these are necessarily wrong, but they leave us with the possibility of using them to bypass the chosen end result which is a personal relationship with the Lord, Himself. Relationships are transformative, and we must be aware of seeking to bypass the requirements of relationship. We will reach the goal of the pathway if we will follow the One who victoriously embraced the pathway Himself.

The Transformation of Our Image

Paul wrote to the Corinthians, "Just as we have borne the image of the earthly [Adam], we will also bear the image of the heavenly [Christ]."[15] The context is Paul's explanation of the transformation of our physical bodies at the final resurrection, but it mirrors the internal, spiritual transformation that takes place in our persons on the moving pathway. We were born in the image of Adam, and we are now being conformed to the image of the Pattern Son. In this mysterious transformation, the process of corruption to which we were enslaved is reversed by the progressive regenerative power of Christ's spirit working in us.[16]

Being transformed into the image of the Son cannot ultimately be accomplished with more and

15   1 Corinthians 15:49
16   See Romans 8:20-21; Ephesians 4:22-24; 1 Peter 1:4.

better teaching, greater discipline, increased moral rectitude, or deeper religious devotion. Each of these may have a certain value, but they can never, in and of themselves, produce the transformation of my entire person.

I believe there are at least three essential and experiential transformations that will be birthed in us as a sovereign work of the Holy Spirit as we allow Jesus to mentor us on the moving pathway. All transformation is the result of Christ's incarnational input. This is His job description!

1. Replacing the fallen mindset with the mind of Christ. The Apostle Paul tells us that renovating our mind[set] is the pathway to transformation.[17] This is of utmost importance for us because, as we noted in the previous *Plumbline,* our mindset is the root of our value system. The fallen mindset can only produce further corruption, but allowing the mind of Christ to be formed in us yields genuine God-life. Not only that, the fallen mindset aggressively rejects the real truth about God and is unable to even comprehend it.[18]

C. Baxter Kruger is a theologian from the Reformed tradition whom I am growing to respect. His description of the fallen mindset is most vivid:

The human race is lost in the most terrible darkness—the darkness of its own fallen

---

17   Romans 12:2.
18   These last two sentences are my paraphrase of Romans 8:6-7.

mind, the darkness of wrong belief and unfaithfulness, of anxiety and projection and misperception. Tragically, the fallen mind is consistent. It never fails. Its dark and anxious imagination creates a false deity, the proof of which it sees everywhere it looks. And this god is very, very real to us, so real that it has become quite "natural" to us, the most obvious thing in the world, the unquestionable truth about divinity, through which we misperceive the heart of the Father without even knowing it.[19]

I especially appreciate Kruger's use of the word "misperceive." What happened to Adam and Eve when their minds were deceived in the fall? Why had the God who gave them life and freely fellowshipped with them suddenly become someone to be feared and from whom they needed to hide? God had not changed. They had entertained the lie and their minds twisted their image of God. That *twisting* of the Father's image has infiltrated religion and many popular views of God.

The mind of Christ perceives and relates to the Father in the same manner Jesus did. The fallen mindset can never truly be transformed by

---

19   *Across All Worlds: Jesus Inside Our Darkness*, by C. Baxter Kruger. Location 689, Kindle edition.

memorizing more Scripture or embracing a better theology. A mindset is too deeply engrained in our being to be changed by cognitive understanding alone. A mindset is more of an attitude—the manner in which we tend to relate or react to others, God, and circumstances. Our understanding must transcend into that which is *meta-cognitive*. This is God's sphere of being—where theory, doctrine, and knowledge transform into an experiential reality. It is where we begin to see and respond as God sees. Our mindset can only genuinely be transformed as we embrace Him who is the Truth. The pathway is calculated to take us where we are not capable of going on our own, revealing elements of our own fallen mindset, and transforming our deepest emotion and reasoning: washing us with the mind of Christ.

2.   *The substance of our faith will be transferred from that which is transactional and cognitive to that which is relational and experiential.* Please hear me when I say that religion (including most of Christianity) is primarily based on that which is transactional and cognitive. It is in our fallen human nature to endeavor to control our worlds and our gods. Transactional religion implies that if we do (or don't do) something, then God will (or won't) do something in response. It is a delusion to believe that if we quote the Bible to God often enough He will do what we want Him to do.

Consider carefully the subtle and deadly differences in these two sets of statements:

> "God blesses me because I live like a Christian should and I am a faithful witness to others." – ***Transactional***

> "I know God loves me because I read it in His Word." – ***Cognitive***

Compare those with:

> "God does only good for me because I am His most beloved daughter / son." – ***Relational***

> "I know God loves me because His Spirit works in me, and I see Him moving on my behalf in all things." – ***Experiential***

A cognitive foundation to our faith is essential, but it is a means to an end and not an end in itself. Knowing more about God is not the same as *knowing* God. Jesus said to the religiously educated of His day, "You have your heads in your Bibles constantly because you think you'll find eternal life there. But you miss the forest for the trees. These Scriptures are all about Me!"[20]

The frightening thing about living relationally is that it can be risky, fluid, unpredictable, and sometimes uncomfortable. The rewards, however, are the experiences of genuine reality: life, joy, adventure, and a matured companionship.

20   John 5:39. *THE MESSAGE: The Bible in Contemporary Language* © 2002 by Eugene H. Peterson.

3. We will become more truly human as God intended. Jesus was not only a revelation of the Father, He was a revelation of what a human person was created to be. As the Pattern Son, He was and is the Pattern Human. If God created Adam and Eve to be humanity in its fullness and pronounced it "very good," then Jesus was also humanity in its fullness as the Last Adam.[21] We tend to think of Jesus taking on human form as necessary for Him to die for sin and to reveal the true nature of the Father. Beyond these aspects of His "job description," He came to *humanize* humanity! Freeing us from a fallen mindset and the enslavement of an eros-driven life, He sets us on a path toward the full glory of our restored humanity for which all creation longingly waits![22]

At the core of becoming truly human is nothing less than a complete and comprehensive change of our personal identity. The human identity that was tied to our fallen state, will now be transferred to being sons and daughters of the Kingdom.[23] All temptation, darkness, and conflict come against our identity, and loss of identity is far more serious than personal sin or failure. We often identify ourselves with our failures, our sin, and our weaknesses: this is our fallen humanity. However, something miraculous and mysterious begins to change in our identity when we come to rest, in the basements of our

---

21 1 Corinthians 15:45.
22 Romans 8:21-22.
23 See Colossians 1:13

being, as daughters and sons in the Agape family of the Father, Christ Jesus, and the Holy Spirit. His desire is to enable us to understand why He has taken us on such a demanding and yet rewarding journey that will involve the recovery of true identity.[24]

The New Birth—An Invitation to Follow Jesus

Evangelical Christianity has traditionally marketed the new birth as the means of assuring eternity in heaven, the forgiveness of sins (at least for provisional forgiveness), and includes a lifetime membership in the "we-try-harder club". I would like to suggest, however, that the new birth is a radical and revolutionary change of our very identities. By way of illustration, suppose that I, Bob Mumford as a younger man, were somehow to awake one morning and find that I had become the member of a semi-nomadic Maasai tribe in Kenya. Beyond the fact that my pale skin would not accommodate the African sun, it would be most difficult for me to adjust to the physically strenuous life style and the new diet. The subtle aspects of language and culture would be beyond me. My genetic heritage and identity from a Northern European lineage would forever cause me to be an alien, frustrated by trying to be someone I am not and continually living outside of the identity of my birth.

---

24   If you are interested in a deeper study of this important topic, consider my Plumbline 334, *Human as God Intended*, from Lifechangers.

In like manner, we were born into this world with the corrupt spiritual "genes" we inherited from the Adamic race. We grow and mature in accordance with that DNA, which is at enmity with God and His Kingdom. To thrive in God's Kingdom we must be reborn by being inseminated with the Agape DNA of Christ. We must be regened or regenerated[25] as it is defined in theology. With new DNA we are truly a *new creation*; one which is totally different from the old. The inability to fully embrace this as experiential reality by relegating it to positional truth has robbed many of their full inheritance in the Kingdom of God. They continue to base their identity in their old person.

To begin to live in a new identity requires that we learn to love and fully embrace the radical unconditional forgiveness, which was made available to us through the resurrection of Christ.[26] This is the irreplaceable foundation of all Kingdom insight and progress on the moving pathway. Most of us learned provisional forgiveness, meaning that we had to live in perpetual confession to keep ourselves right with God. Provisional forgiveness issues out of the fallen mindset that sees God as continually keeping

---

25 "Regeneration, or new birth, is an inner re-creating of fallen human nature by the gracious sovereign action of the Holy Spirit." (Baker's Dictionary of Theology, P. 440. Baker Book House, 1973.

26 Please note 1 Corinthians 15:16-17, which indicates that only in the resurrection of Christ was full forgiveness of sin made effectual.

a checklist of our sins and crossing them off only when we have repented and asked for forgiveness. Tragically, we will continue to be sin-focused rather than Father-focused because with each repetition of confession there is a reminder of our sin day after day.[27]

With radical forgiveness, we embrace Father's desire and intent to redeem the innocence that was lost through exploring the knowledge of good and evil. He will again allow us to eat freely from the fruit of the Tree of Life, the Agape outflow from the sweet society of the Trinity. Try reading again Paul's thoughts on our relation to sin in the sixth chapter of Romans considering it as an *experiential reality.* If understood and embraced it is truly radical and world shattering!

Please, please don't miss the revolutionary fact that our sin was dealt with before the foundation of the world! The Father's resolve to reconcile us, and all creation, to Himself is predicated on this magnificent reality. His plan for reconciliation could never have become effectual if He was continually "counting our trespasses against us."[28]

Please hear me carefully. If we cannot embrace and personalize radical forgiveness, then we will leave an open door to all manner of accusation, condemnation, guilt, and discouragement. The forces of

27   See Hebrews 10:2-3 to understand that the cleansing of the perfect sacrifice should take our focus away from sin.

28   2 Corinthians 5:19

darkness, the dogmas of transactional religion, and our own fallen consciences will hurl against us. If we are capable of embracing radical forgiveness, then the inevitable missteps, weaknesses, and shortcomings that are manifested by design on the moving pathway will no longer be a source of self-condemnation and defeat. They will become the opportunities to lean further into the empowering grace of the new birth, which becomes transformative.

The new birth also spiritually equips us in two ways. First we are empowered to recognize, embrace, and respond to the unexpected happenings in life. The Scriptures never promise escape from the stress and pains of life. Jesus did not ask for us to be taken out of the world,[29] and in fact stated that our walk in this life would contain a measure of pressure and conflict. As we put on the mind of Christ we begin to understand those very storms are part of the "all things" of the moving pathway. There seems to be no escaping them—I fervently wish there was!

Secondly, we are now being equipped to thrive in and enjoy God's spiritual, meta-physical sphere – His governmental realm. This is who we are created to become! All our spiritual senses are enlivened, giving us the ability to see His glory, hear His voice, live in His Agape, and understand His mind and ways! This is beyond the capacity of our natural senses and understanding, but through the new birth we are impregnated with the Holy Spirit who gifts

29   John 17:15

us with the revelation and grace to live in the world of spirit. We simply cannot follow Him unless and until He equips us to do so!

As we are born into the spiritual realm, we are presented with His Kingdom offer: unreservedly commit to following Jesus on the moving pathway; present ourselves to God for His purposes, which lead us toward our inheritance in the Kingdom. This invitation is offered within the context of water baptism, signifying the inexorable requirement of our willingness to bury in death all that would detract from entering into that sweet society of fellowship in the Trinity. All forms of corruption, known and unknown, are assigned to death and burial, and we are raised up to walk in newness of life. Water baptism, when understood in governmental terms, takes on the form of spiritual warfare. We bury all that accuses, torments, and seeks to drag us back down into the corruption from which we have been set free! This is made possible by yielding our *personal sovereignty*. There is no other way our freedom can be accomplished.

If you have not done so, I would again encourage you to carefully read Romans chapter six, not as positional theology but as a living experience into which you are called for God's eternal purposes!

Jesus' Job Description

Simply stated, Jesus job description as given by His Father is to redeem us from the ever-present torment and captivity of the fallen mindset and to bring us to the Father. My conviction is that religion has corrupted the origin and purpose of the redemptive act making it to be heaven, rather than the biblical goal of our being reconciled into a living relationship with the Father. We must be abundantly and redundantly clear that when Jesus declared that He was "the Way" to the Father He was not primarily talking about a place (heaven) nor a positional, legal remedy to our problem of sin. The Father desires an experiential revelation as He truly is and a renewed relationship for which we were created.

This was initiated at Jesus' resurrection in what I have come to understand as a *redemptive event horizon*. In the world of physics, an event horizon is a boundary in time-space beyond which events on one side can no longer affect an observer on the opposite side. It is a point of no return. When Christ rose from the dead the work of the cross was applied to all creation with radical forgiveness.[30] Radical forgiveness is not a process—it is a completed act of God's grace that was foreseen and initiated before the foundation of the world. It was applied to all creation (which includes the entire race)[31] at the event horizon of Jesus' resurrection.

Lest this seem too radical, consider carefully what Paul writes to the Corinthians, "God was in Christ *reconciling the world* to Himself, *not count-*

---

30   See 1 Corinthians 15:17.
31   See John 1:29; 1 John 2:2.

ing their trespasses against them, and He has committed to us the word of reconciliation [emphasis mine]."[32]

Here are two important points of logic in Paul's statement. First, why was God not counting the world's trespasses against them? They had been radically forgiven—their trespasses were no longer the primary issue! Second, anyone who has ever dealt with conflict or wounding resulting in a rift in relationship is aware that before the relationship can be reconciled there must be forgiveness of the wrongs which were done: forgiveness *must* proceed reconciliation. Reconciliation of the world was being put into effect through Christ; forgiveness had to have been a foregone reality in God's posture toward the world.

The event horizon of Jesus' resurrection "put away [disannulled, abolished] sin" for all time. [33] If we cannot fully embrace this reality we will forever be going round and round like a dog chasing its tail. We will incessantly be striving for a sense of freedom from a nagging sense of inadequacy. We must lay hold of the fact that our short-comings, missteps, and failures have already been factored into our journey. They become occasions for our growth and maturity rather than occasions for guilt and self-frustration. Part of our problem has come from the religious teaching about sin that tends to <u>focus on mora</u>lity and ethics in thought, word, and

32 2 Corinthians 5:19
33 Hebrews 9:26

deed. The Greek word, *harmartia*, which is always translated "sin," is best translated "miss the mark."[34] With this in mind it should become evident that when we "sin" we are ultimately failing to hit the mark of the glory of the Son[35]. The Father's intent is not to punish or cut us off when we fail; rather, it is to encourage and strengthen us to go at it again.

The new birth with water baptism as it is presented in the New Testament is designed to be a personal event horizon. The old is buried with Christ, and we have passed through a point of no return. The events occurring in the past can no longer affect us. The new birth and water baptism introduces us to the moving pathway with the intent of our becoming a living incarnation of the eternal value system in the same manner as Jesus. The moving pathway is designed as a pathway of failure and success (without guilt, condemnation, or separation) until we get it right, hitting the mark rather than missing it.

Fully Persuaded

Jesus sees to it that we are fully persuaded that the moving pathway is not only the way, but the only way to the Father. God is not interested in

34 I recognize that there are other types of sin besides missing the mark. However, transgression and iniquity are more volitional in nature. It is our failures due to the fleshly nature as it relates to living by the eternal value system that will be the focus of our study.

35 See Romans 3:23

being another Caesar. He seeks to persuade us that living by the eternal value system will be worth any price or sacrifice. Agape does not coerce or force itself upon us. God, as a Father, approaches us somewhat indirectly to persuade us to consider and embrace the Kingdom offer. Here is a most eloquent and accurate expression of the Father's ways by George McDonald, the great Scottish author and apologist of the 1800's:

> Nor will God force any door to enter in. He may send a tempest about the house; the wind of His admonishment may burst the doors and windows, yes, shake the house to its foundations, but not then, not so, will He enter. The door must be opened by the willing hand, ere the foot of Love will cross the threshold. He watches to see the door move from within. Every tempest is but an assault of the siege of Love. The terror of God is but the other side of His Love; it is love outside, that would be inside—Love that knows the house is no house, only a place, until it enters.[36]

The flow of compelling events is designed to persuade us that the Kingdom is the only way to live. To understand the necessity of being fully per-

---

[36] *George MacDonald, An Anthology* by CS Lewis, pg.44. © 1946, by C. S. Lewis Pte. Ltd.

suaded to stay the course on the moving pathway as the only real option, I would like to draw on the example of Abraham who is the father of all who walk in faith. When Abram left the Ur of the Chaldees he stepped onto the moving pathway. The goal was for him to become the father of many nations and for all the nations of the earth would be blessed in him. In Romans chapter four, Paul makes the statement that Abraham "found" something. What did he find? Paul is using Abraham as an example of one who was justified by faith because God counted Abraham's faith as righteousness. Paul quotes from Genesis 15:6, when he writes, "Abraham believed God, and it was credited to him as righteousness." I would like you to consider that righteousness means "right standing *relationally*." It is not only a legal statement but also a relational statement. Abraham would find that if he would love God, He would absorb his failures and walk with him.

Paul's commentary on Abraham through the rest of this chapter shows Abraham became "fully persuaded"[37] that God would fulfill His promise to give him a son even though he regarded his own body "as good as dead" and the "deadness of Sarah's womb." In other words Abraham believed that God would bring about some form of *resurrection* in his and Sarah's bodies in order for them to have the promised child. Abraham would later be asked by God to offer Isaac as a sacrifice. He was willing

---

37 Romans 4:21 (Young's Literal Translation).

to obey because "he considered that God is able to raise people even from the dead."[38] In some manner Abraham had come to understand that embracing the death of obedience was the pathway to God's promise of resurrection. Ultimately Abraham was able to choose Isaac's death rather than disobey God. Because of Abraham's most difficult act of obedience the blessing of Abraham has been offered to all the families and nations of the earth.

Here is one of the most urgent challenges we must embrace if we are to mature on the moving pathway: we must be willing to embrace personal death. We cannot cling to self-preservation but rather look to God's resurrection in all situations of life. This defines the meaning of water baptism; it is more than symbol.

As the Father's moving pathway proceeds, we will encounter situations that by design will require we release our white-knuckle grip on self-preservation, trusting in a resurrection through the working of God's power. As we experience the death of obedience, we learn that resurrection will come by the work of Father's grace. We become fully persuaded that the moving path is the only way to freedom and a living relationship.

I am reminded of God's statement through Moses to Israel as they were about to enter the Promised Land after their deliverance and forty years wandering in the wilderness [*think: moving pathway!*]:

38 Hebrews 11:19.

In the wilderness He fed you manna which your fathers did not know, that He might humble you and that He might test you, *to do good for you in the end* [Italics mine].[39]

In the wilderness one generation died and a new one was resurrected that was willing to obey God and possess their inheritance. It is an inviolate principle of the Universe that nothing is transformed except by death and resurrection.

If we are fully persuaded that the ultimate goal of genuine transformation is not just an option but the only option, we will step onto the pathway without looking back or embracing the option to go our own way. Jesus warned those who were following him that they should carefully consider the moving pathway and be prepared to stay the course.[40]

I have been fascinated by the grueling training that Navy SEALS must undergo to earn the coveted insignia—the gold trident pin. Especially torturous is hell week which may eliminate up to half of those who begin. During this week they will only be allowed to sleep four hours a night and will be wet, cold, and pushed to extreme physical limits continually. Those who succeed are not always the strongest or biggest, but it is those for whom quitting is simply not an option. During hell week, SEAL candidates are free to quit at any time by simply walk-

---

39 Deuteronomy 8:16
40 Consider reading Jesus discourse in Luke 14:26-33.

ing away from the group where they will be greeted by instructors with a blanket and cup of hot coffee. They will then ring a brass bell announcing that they have chosen to leave and head for a hot shower and rest. They are never shamed or ridiculed, they simply return to continue serving in their former duty.

In like manner, Jesus desires those who are persuaded to stay on the pathway without a sense of compulsion or guilt, those who are desirous of growth by facing life's challenges "for the joy" of enduring, overcoming, and being transformed. They are those for whom ringing the bell is not an option. After Jesus had delivered a rather difficult discourse and many followers began to leave Him, He turned to His disciples and ask them if they wanted to leave as well. It was an open invitation to "ring the brass bell." "No," they said, "You're the only one with Life; we've no place else to go."[41]

In the end, and at all points in between, we face a similar choice. We either embrace the life-giving and liberating pain of our enlightenment in Jesus, which gives way to sheer joy in the Father's embrace, or we continue to live in our own worlds, where our way of seeing things produces deeper and deeper alienation, brokenness, and misery.

Allow me to quote Paul's description of his own embrace of the moving pathway while adding comments relating to our present theme.

---

41   See John 6:66-69.

But whatever things were gain to me, those things I have counted as loss for the sake of Christ *[Paul had given up his personal value system for the eternal value system]*. More than that, I count all things to be loss in view of the surpassing value of knowing Christ Jesus my Lord, for whom I have suffered the loss of all things, and count them but rubbish so that I may gain Christ, and may be found in Him, not having a righteousness of my own derived from the Law, but that which is through faith in Christ, the righteousness *[He seeks a relational righteousness]* which comes from God on the basis of faith, that I may know Him *[This is the treasure in the field for which Paul "sold all he had"]* and the power of His resurrection and the fellowship of His sufferings, being conformed to His death *[Willing to embrace the all things of the moving pathway]*; in order that I may attain to the resurrection *[literal: out-resurrection]* from the dead.

Not that I have already obtained it or have already become perfect, but I press on *[Continual embrace of the moving pathway]* so that I may lay hold of that for which also I was laid hold of by Christ Jesus *[to know the Agape of Christ]*. Brethren, I do not regard myself as laving laid hold of it yet; but one thing I do: forgetting what lies behind and reaching forward to what lies ahead, I press on toward the goal for the prize of the upward call of God in Christ Jesus. Let us therefore, as many as are perfect *[mature is a better meaning]*, have this attitude *[a mindset, value system, or affection]*; and if in anything you have a different attitude, God will reveal that also to you; however, let us keep living by that same standard to which we have attained (Philippians 3:7-14).

I believe the prize for which Paul sought was not ministry, anointing, or recognition but the Agape of Christ Himself. He clearly understood that all things on the moving pathway could involve death and resurrection, but the joy over discovering the treasure in the field or purchasing the pearl of great price was worth giving up all that he had.

The "out-resurrection" Paul was striving to attain is unique in the language of the New Testament: *exanastasis*. He does not have in view the eventual bodily resurrection of the dead, rather, a resurrection that may be experienced as an outcome of the moving pathway. *Vine's Expository Dictionary of the New Testament Words* translates this phrase "the out-resurrection from among the dead." It is not a resurrection from a state of death, rather a resurrection from among dead things. It is freedom from the entanglements and distractions of the Seven Giants; the freedom to grow and bear fruit based on our radical forgiveness and the spiritual empowerment of the new birth.

Here's how Jesus expressed the moving pathway to His followers:

Then Jesus went to work on his disciples. "Anyone who intends to come with me has to let me lead. You're not in the driver's seat; I am. Don't run from suffering; embrace it. Follow me and I'll show you how. Self-help is no help at all. Self-sacrifice is the way, my way, to finding yourself, your true self. What kind of deal is it to get everything you want but lose yourself? What could you ever trade your soul for?"[42]

Restoring Our Responsibility

A clear understanding and acceptance of human responsibility is in desperate need of restoration. The absolute foundation of restored human responsibility is *choice*. Simply stated, choice constitutes our human responsibility on the Moving pathway. As we encounter all things we will be presented with "forced choices." By that I mean that we will encounter situations, people, and circumstances where we have no option but to

---

42   Matthew 16:24-26. THE MESSAGE: The Bible in Contemporary Language © 2002 by Eugene H. Peterson.

make a choice. Our choices may be summarized as follows:

- eternal value system (Agape) vs. corrupted value system (eros)
- willing to count all as lost vs. self-preservation

The eros choice that is immediate and self-fulfilling leads to death and loss of inheritance. In contrast is our choice of Agape, which seeks to build our life by means of the eternal value system, resulting in increased life, joy, and the embrace of the Father's pleasure.

There is a fire on the moving pathway that will reveal our choice as gold, silver, precious stones or wood, hay, and straw.[43] At this point we must be exceedingly clear: the fire of God is purifying, not punitive; it is restorative, not retributive! "Death" is not punishment from God, it is a natural consequence of going our own way. N.T. Wright, an English theologian, expresses the distinction:

> It ought to be clear from all this that the reason "sin" leads to "death" is not at all (as is often supposed) that "death" is an arbitrary and somewhat draconian punishment for miscellaneous moral shortcomings. The link is deeper than that. The distinction I am making is like the distinction between the ticket you will get if you are caught driving too fast and the crash that will happen if you

---

43   1 Corinthians 3:11-15

drive too fast around a sharp bend on a wet road. The ticket is arbitrary, an imposition with no organic link to the offense. The crash is intrinsic, the direct consequence of the behavior. In the same way, death is the intrinsic result of sin, not simply an arbitrary punishment.[44]

Forgiveness is not an issue. We will be given repeated "forced choices" until we are able to begin to choose based on the eternal value system. Failure is part of God presenting us with opportunities to lean into Him, grow, mature, and ultimately bear fruit.

As Israel was about to enter the Land under Joshua, Moses challenged them:

> I call heaven and earth to witness against you today, that I have set before you life and death, the blessing and the curse. So *choose* life in order that you may live.[45]

The challenge of all things on the moving pathway is the same for each of us choose life or death; the eternal value system or the corrupt value system of self-preservation. The fruit of the corrupt value system is seen in every area of life today: personal lives, families, economics, international relations, social strife, and environmental devastation.

44   Wright, N. T. *The Day the Revolution Began;* P. 86. HarperOne. Kindle Edition.

45   Deuteronomy 30:19

How to Respond

When challenges arise on the moving pathway in the form of problems, there are five possible responses, each of which appears as a perfectly normal solution. Once difficulty exists, our choice can detour us from our objective. The result is the injury or delay of the process of transformation.

The first reaction is to *deny*. "De-nial" is not a river in Egypt! Denial is alive and well in the larger body of Christ. All of us have experienced going into denial at one time or another. Often denial is

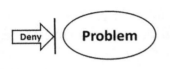

expressed by, "What problem? I don't have a problem. It's my husband / wife / boss who has the problem!" All the while everyone else is very much aware of the elephant sitting in the room.

Denial is best illustrated by Sarah's famous laugh at the word of the Angel that she would have a child. It was a pure form of denial. This *cannot* be, and she gave all of the reasons. It will not be, for she is not sure she will co-operate. Her mind rebels: God can do many things, but this is too much. Personally, I too, have experienced clear denial on several occasions, only to hear the Lord say, "More than you can ask or think."[46]

The second is to *avoid*. We very carefully work our way around the problem and continue on our

---

46   Ephesians 3:20

own way because we do not want or think we have the equipment to deal with the problem.

Avoidance, of course, is another form of denial,

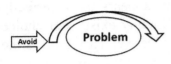

but much more subtle. It is playing intellectual and emotional games with ourselves for the purpose of getting our own way. We seek to avoid people, issues, problems, and certain conversations. Circumvention becomes an acquired skill as contrasted to developing the skill of abiding and skipping the detour.

A third response is to *endure*. We enter the circumstance but do so with deep, internal resistance. This is why we actually survive the time factor, yet

we remain unaffected or unchanged. We are describing how a person can survive four years in

the military or ten years in prison without benefit or personal change. He or she simply endures in prison. All they are concerned about is doing the time. Many people endure marriage in a similar manner. We do not yield or seek to discover what could change; we simply endure year after year. Application to our Christian experience should be self-evident. We can endure Sunday morning, prayer, and Bible reading with an attitude of waiting until this is over. We have missed the intimacy our Lord is offering in His redemptive act and the unbelievable offer of

His friendship[47].

The fourth one is to *turn back*. This one is more drastic. This is what Israel tried to do coming out of Egypt because they missed the leeks and the onions. I met the Lord dramatically at the age of twelve. However, because of the ridicule of family and friends I decided I did not want to go on into this new and unexplored world of the Kingdom of God. As a result, I turned back. That led to twelve years as a backslider until the Lord graciously reclaimed me. Few things give us a clearer insight into the twisted nature of fallen man than a clear insight into how easily we can turn back after all the demonstration of God's Love in the Person of Christ. Paul asks the Galatian believers, "But now that you have come to know God, or rather to be known by God, how is it that you *turn back again* to the weak and worthless elemental things, to which you desire to be enslaved all over again?"[48]

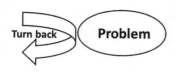

Embrace and abide is the fifth response, and the alternative to all four of these responses. All others present themselves to us as

---

47   John 15:15
48   Galatians 4:9

sophisticated occasions to run, hide, and shift blame. The only way through is embrace and abide. This is Jesus' prescription in John 15:7-10:

> If you abide in Me, and My words abide in you, ask whatever you wish, and it shall be done for you. "By this is My Father glorified, that you bear much fruit, and so prove to be My disciples." Just as the Father has loved (Agape) Me, I have also loved (Agape) you; abide in My love (Agape).

When we are in the middle of a problem or circumstances that we would prefer to avoid or when everything within us wants to deny what is happening, we must see that abiding is the only manner in which we can embrace the situation. When we are gritting our teeth and pressures are multiplying and telling us we had better turn back or we will perish in the wilderness, it is then we need to say, "Father, I am Yours. You know I believe You are able to work all things together for good because I love You. My focus is on You. You are the object of my affection." It is only our love for God in response to His love for us that makes the circumstances unfold and serve the purposes of God in our life.

My ongoing sense of the Father's love (Agape) believes that we can ask our way out of a set of circumstances in which the Father would prefer us to abide. He does use all things, even our insistence for Him to do what He would prefer not to do at the time. Father knows the end from the beginning and due to His knowledge of the long-term results, He would have preferred us to abide, but honors our insistent and determined prayer for release.

Foundational Choices

Each time we choose to embrace the eternal value system there are three foundational choices required to fully follow through on the choice.

First, we must choose to hear His voice and learn the wisdom of discernment. If we are not sure of the way and we have a guide, it may be wise to listen to what he has to say.

In my younger days I was an avid hunter. One of my most memorable trips was deep into the wilds of Bob Marshall Wilderness in northwestern Montana. It is more than one million acres; massive, breathtaking, remote, and very rugged. The range we needed to cover was too expansive to hunt on foot, so our guide took the four of us deep into the wilderness with horses to help us traverse the necessary distances. He gave me a horse that was providentially and prophetically named "Chief."

One afternoon I chose the direction of my day's hunt and confidently started out with Chief. I became overly intent on trailing a big bull elk and as a result became totally disoriented as to my location. Gradually I began to be alarmed because if I did not find camp by nightfall I could be in serious trouble because the nights were exceedingly cold.

Finally, I was pretty sure our camp was off to my right. I reigned Chief that direction, but he continually baulked as I tried to lead him that way. Ultimately, I had enough wisdom to realize perhaps Chief knew more about this wilderness than I did. I released the reigns and said, "Okay, Chief, take us back to camp." He immediately turned the opposite direction and started off. Everything in me knew he was heading the wrong way! He headed down an incredibly steep incline, so steep that I had to hold onto the back of the saddle to keep from going over his head. He got to the bottom, turned right, went around a hill, and there was the camp. I almost burst into tears.

That night around the campfire I said to the guide, "I am amazed you would trust me to go out by myself in this wilderness."

He laughed, "I don't trust you—*I trust Chief*!"

Jesus is our guide, and the Holy Spirit is our Chief. Jesus cannot always trust us to make correct choices, but He does trust the Holy Spirit if we will choose to let Him do the leading!

Hearing His voice is a skill we must actively and aggressively cultivate. To hear His voice we must first have a heart to hear His voice, as Jesus often said, "He who has an ear to hear, let him hear." This necessitates a desire to obey rather than to go our own way.

A man whom I pastored for many years told

of seeking the Lord about a difficult situation that seemed to have no answer. One day when he asked the Lord again how he should handle the situation the Lord answered, "I won't tell you because if I did you wouldn't do it!" He would have been unable to obey because he valued self-preservation over obedience.

We must also know His voice of wisdom to properly respond to each challenge we will face on the moving pathway. Some situations may be demonic in origin, which we must rebuke and overcome by our authority in Christ because they are opposing us and the work of God. Jesus rebuked Satan, the storm on the sea, and demons when they opposed Him or tormented the people. We are told by the New Testament that we are to wrestle, overcome, pull down, and resist the powers of darkness. All of these concepts are included in the Kingdom concept of learning to transcend everything and everyone that seeks to cause us to go the wrong way.

Other situations we must avoid or remove ourselves from because to remain there will lead to our defeat or spiritual harm. When Jesus was about to be stoned, He hid himself from the crowd and left the temple. On another occasion He eluded those who were seeking to seize Him, and for a season He refused to minister in Judea because the Jews were seeking to kill Him. Likewise we are told to flee lusts; avoid corrupt persons and bad company; and not to associate with works of darkness. Some things we cannot rebuke, overpower, or endure; we just need to remove ourselves!

Sometimes the moving pathway seems to stop and all progress in spiritual growth appears to come to a screeching halt. These dry times when God seems silent and unresponsive can often prove to be some of the most fruitful in the long run. If we have the wisdom to discern these times as part of "all things" then we know it is a time when we must endure, wait patiently, hope against hope, not cast away our confidence, hold fast, and keep looking. It is a season when our "wine" is aging, our fruit is ripening and our faith is being refined. Discern these seasons and treasure them!

We will encounter many situations on the moving pathway that will be part of the all things that are worked by God for our ultimate good. We must face and embrace them, seeking to please the Father by responding out of the eternal value system as Jesus did in Gethsemane. Learning the when and the how is dependent on our ability to hear His voice and discern His direction.

Second, we chose to engage a life of "repentance." I put repentance in quotation marks because I intend to use it in a non-traditional manner. I even hesitate to use this term because it is loaded with centuries of religious baggage that is in no way consistent with the New Testament in either language or intent. Repentance as it has been handed down to us from the Middle Ages is focused on sin, behavior, and repeatedly seeking forgiveness. It conjures up visions of sleepless monks flagellating themselves in their cells or guilty sinners weeping out their regret and remorse before God's imminent displeasure.

When carefully examined, repentance as it is used in the New Testament is used in connection with a single choice or a series of choices in which there is a change of mindset or values resulting in a change of life style. Repentance is not fixated on sin. It is focused on changing our mindset and continually turning away from fear, doubt, condemnation, and dead works. The power of these negative thoughts will choke our joy and peace, leaving us feeling as if we are spiritual failures. Paul says:

> Finally, believers, whatever is true, whatever is honorable and worthy of respect, whatever is right and confirmed by God's word, whatever is pure and wholesome, whatever is lovely and brings peace, whatever is admirable and of good repute; if there is any excellence, if there is anything worthy of praise, think continually on these things [center your mind on them, and implant them in your heart].[49]

A man was watching Monday night football when his grey tabby cat began rubbing his leg soliciting some attention. Not wanting to lose

---

49 Philippians 4:8. Amplified.

sight of the action he reached down and without looking began to pet his cat, beginning from the tail and stroking toward the head. The cat found this less than pleasing and protested with a loud "EEEEOOOOWWW!"

Being more concerned about the Patriot's drive toward a winning touchdown, he continued to stroke the cat in the same manner, provoking the same response from the cat.

"EEEEOOOOWWW!"

"EEEEOOOOWWW!"

"EEEEOOOOWWW!"

Finally, greatly irritated by the continued squalling, he snapped at the cat, "What's the matter with you?!"

The cat hissed back, "You're rubbing my fur the wrong direction!"

"Well," the man said, "TURN AROUND!"

This silly story captures the essence of repentance. It is quite simply a decision to turn around, and in the language of the New Testament it relates primarily to our mind set and not sin or sins. The Greek word for repentance is *metanoia,* which literally means to "a change of mind or intention" or "come think with me." We are seeking to implement *metanoia* as an urgent element for our continuing growth and maturity in the manner presented in the New Testament. One Bible paraphrase translates *metanoia* as "align your thinking with Christ."[50] In

50   The Mirror Bible. © 2012 by Francois du Toit.

putting on the mind of Christ we cease to dwell in sin consciousness and focus on pleasing the Father. The author of Hebrews tells us that "repentance from dead works" is foundational to moving on to maturity[51]. In other words, if we refuse or are unable to leave the religious, fallen mind set that continually focuses on personal failures and best efforts, we will never be able to live in freedom, poised joyfully toward the Father and embracing the eternal value system.

Third, we must choose to become comfortable with mystery. We said earlier that the moving pathway is a mystery. It is, however, part of a larger eternal mystery—*the Mystery of Christ Himself.* The Cosmic Christ is the Mystery of all creation, "in whom are hidden all the treasures of wisdom and knowledge."[52]

We are all drawn to mystery. It is something engrained deep in our spiritual persons; it is eternity hidden in our hearts. Without knowing it our draw to Mystery is a longing to know the Mystery—the Cosmic Christ. This internal wonder of Mystery is why science passionately seeks to discover the mysteries of the universe, its origins, the beginning of life, and our own being. Why seek the beginning, the source, the unmoved mover, the intellect that moves the cosmos? Perhaps it is because we know that if we discover these mysteries it will in some

---

51 Hebrews 6:1
52 Colossians 2:3

measure enable us to answer the cosmic why: who we are and why we came to be—it will give us *identity*. Perhaps we are searching to find ourselves in the One "in whom we live and move and have out being."[53]

God does hide Himself and His ways in mystery. He reserves for Himself the right to not "cast His pearls before swine".[54] Deuteronomy tells us that mysteries must be revealed or given by God. If we seek after the hidden things beyond what has been given we are in danger of going down the path of darkness. The powers of darkness are willing to give revelation to those who seek after it apart from a relationship with the living God. The revealing of mystery brings relationship and attachment. If God gives revelation, we partake of His life. In contrast if it is darkness giving revelation, then we partake of its life producing confusion and consternation.

Failure to embrace and become comfortable with the mysterious conundrums of the moving pathway is one of the major reasons people stumble [scandalized], fall away from the faith, or choose to live their lives with an underlying anger or resentment toward God. Our theology (cognitive) tells us God is good, loving, and caring, but our innermost person may be left tenuous, unsure of God's love, and unwilling to unreservedly commit ourselves into his providential Fatherhood in every aspect of our lives.

53 Acts 17:28
54 Matthew 7:6

To be comfortable with Mystery is to be comfortable with God being Himself without our permission or understanding! It is letting go of the need to be to know and control. Choosing to be comfortable with Mystery means that we will come to rest in the infinite nature and character of Agape in the Trinity. It is Agape, as the all-encompassing force that holds the Universe, history and our own lives on a course, moving us toward God being restored as All in All.

Please seek to enjoy the romance and adventure of Mystery. It is not God resisting our curiosity; He is using mystery to draw us ever more intimately into Himself and His eternal being. Kingdom is relational and seldom functions as transactional.

Choice: it is ours minute by minute, day by day, year by year. It is the glorious freedom and privilege God has given us to *choose life—that we might live!*

His goal is to make us living incarnations of the eternal value system.

- We will keep our word.
- We will not encroach on that which is another's.
- We will seek to do good to all.
- If we cannot do good, we will refuse to do harm.

Conclusion: Refuse to ring the bell!

Remember the Navy SEALs who always had the option to ring the bell and leave the excruciating physical and psychological pressures of hell week? Only those for whom quitting was not an option would ultimately win the prize. They know how to *endure*. The Greek word for endure signifies: "to be left standing after all others have collapsed."

In the spiritual economy of the Kingdom, endurance is an end in itself. James tells us that the moving pathway produces endurance and we may then "let endurance have its perfect result, that we might be perfect and complete, lacking in nothing!"[55]

Please indulge me as I once again insert this most poignant cartoon! I would encourage you to meditate on it from time to time. Seldom has anything allowed me to see more clearly into the distinction between the "ideal" and the real!

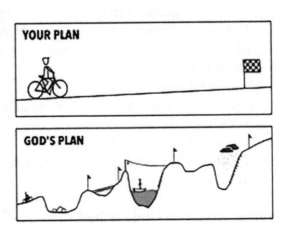

---

55 James 1:2

My most sincere prayer for each of you is that by grasping some measure of the moving pathway, you will be enabled to press on toward that for which Christ called you, becoming a living incarnation of the eternal value system!

What next? We are not merely destined to be conformed into the image of the Son, we are commissioned to incarnate and manifest that image before a stumbling and hurting world. We are called to be part of *The Third Incarnation*, which will be the topic of our next *Plumbline!*

 ®

P.O. Box 3709 ❖ Cookeville, TN 38502
931.520.3730 ❖ lc@lifechangers.org

CPSIA information can be obtained
at www.ICGtesting.com
Printed in the USA
LVHW080752091219
639682LV00012B/9/P